624

Pyramids

Fiona Macdonald

FRANKLIN WATTS
LONDON • SYDNEY

First published in 2000 by
Franklin Watts
96 Leonard Street
London
EC2A 4XD

Franklin Watts Australia
14 Mars Road
Lane Cove
NSW 2066

Copyright © Franklin Watts 2000

ISBN 0 7496 3702 1

Dewey Decimal
Classification Number: 624

A CIP catalogue for this book is
available from the British Library

Printed in Hong Kong/China

Series editor: Anderley Moore
Series designer: John Christopher, WHITE DESIGN
Picture research: Sue Mennell
Illustrators: Peter Bull, Virginia Gray, Sarah John, The
Maltings Partnership

Cover: Werner Forman Archive / Dr E. Strouhal; AKG /
Robert O'Dea (inset)

Interior Pictures:
Illustrations: Peter Bull: pp.6-7 (bottom), p.9, p.11; Virginia
Gray: 8; Sarah John: p.15, p.20, pp.28-29; The Maltings
Partnership: pp. 6-7 (main image), p.14, p.19.
Photography: AKG: 11 (Henning Bock), p.22 (top) Robert
O'Dea, p.25 (top) Erich Lessing, p.27 (Gilles Mermet);
The Ancient Egypt Picture library: p.7; Axiom: p.22
(bottom) M. Winch, p.24 (James Morris); Ecoscene: p.26
(Sally Morgan); SCALA Picture Library: p.18; Still
Pictures: p.12 (bottom); Sylvia Cordaiy: 16 (Guy Marks),
p.23 (Paul Kaye); Travel Ink: p.13 (top) Abbie Enock, p.13
(bottom) John Grant, p.21 (top) Mark Reeve, p.21
(bottom) Simon Reddy, p.25 (bottom) Sean Evison, p.28
(Christine Pemberton); Werner Forman Archive: p.4-5
(Dr E. Strouhal), p.10, p.12 (top), p.17 (National Museum
of Anthropology, Mexico City), p.19 (Pigorini Museum
of Prehistory and Ethnography, Rome), p.27.

Contents

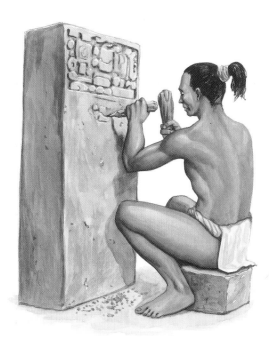
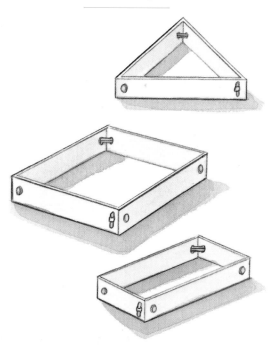

What is a pyramid?

Beautiful, huge mysterious – these are just some of the words used to describe the pyramids of Ancient Egypt. People long ago named the pyramids one of the seven 'Wonders of the World'. They have intrigued and astounded people for centuries and they still attract thousands of tourists today.

Number work

The mathematical definition of a pyramid is 'a many-sided shape where all the sides are triangles'. The base can be a triangle, or a different shape.

How many different types of pyramid can you draw?

What are pyramids?

Pyramids are tall, pointed mounds, usually made of earth or stone. Some are over 100 metres high. The most famous pyramids are in Egypt, a country in North Africa. They were built between 3000 and 1000 BC.

➡ *These pyramids at Giza in Egypt were built for Pharaoh Khufu and members of his family around 2500 BC.*

Pyramid words

Many different words are used to describe pyramid building in this book. Can you find the ones below and discover what they mean?

base	core
apex	rubble
capstone	slope
casing	burial chamber
foundation	face
ziggurat	

Who built the pyramids?

The Egyptian pyramids were built by gangs of workmen, obeying commands given by the pharaohs (kings) who ruled ancient Egypt. They were constructed of stone blocks laid over a core of rubble (rough lumps of earth and stone).

Most pyramids were designed as burial chambers; they have tombs inside. But over the centuries, pyramids have proved such tempting targets for robbers that most of the treasures they once contained have been removed.

Did you know...

The Ancient Egyptian word for pyramid was 'mer'. Our word 'pyramid' comes from 'pyramis', the Ancient Greek word for 'wheat-cake'. This is because the Greeks used to eat little mound-shaped cakes, made of wheat and honey. They also gave them as offerings to their gods. Travellers from Ancient Greece visited Egypt, and gave the pyramid buildings there the same Greek name as their cakes!

The first pyramids

The first Egyptian pyramid was built around 2,650 BC, at Saqqara. It was designed as a tomb for Pharaoh Djoser. It probably began as a flat, box-like structure, which was later redesigned. Six 'steps' were built, one above the other, to create a pyramid shape.

The Saqqara pyramid set a fashion. Before long, other step pyramids were built to cover pharaohs' tombs. These later pyramids often had smooth, sloping sides added, to cover the step-structure underneath.

Timeline: Pyramids in Egypt

3100–2181 BC
Flat boxes or mastabas built to cover tombs

2667–2648 BC
First step pyramid

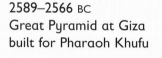

2648–2640 BC
First true pyramid; also the 'bent' pyramid

2589–2566 BC
Great Pyramid at Giza built for Pharaoh Khufu

2494–2345 BC
Pharaohs begin to spend money on temples rather than pyramids

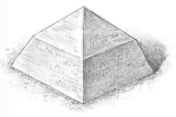

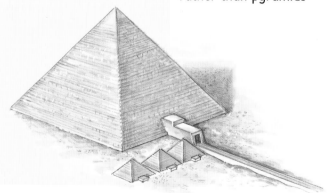

◀ Once the steps of the pyramid were built, workers smoothed over them to form slopes.

Pyramid building

It took excellent building skills and accurate calculations to construct a pyramid. The first true pyramid was built around 2613–2589 BC for Pharaoh Sneferu. The 'bent' pyramid at Dahshur was also built at about this time. After around 2490 BC, pharaohs began to spend money on funeral temples, rather than pyramids.

▲ The bent pyramid got its name because its sides do not slope evenly.

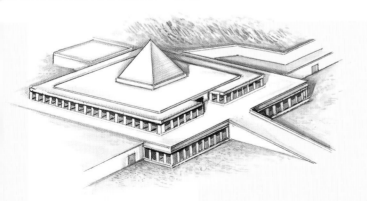

2055–2004 BC
Pharaoh Mentuhotep builds small pyramid on top of temple

1985–1650 BC
Pyramids made of cheap mud brick, not expensive stone

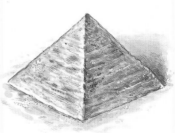

1550–1525 BC
Pharaoh Ahmose I builds memorial shaped like a pyramid

c 1500 - 1000 BC
Pyramids built on top of funeral chapels

c 1000 BC
No more pyramids built in Egypt

A special shape

Pyramids are a special shape, unlike anything else on earth. To the ancient Egyptians, this shape had three special meanings:

First of all, the pyramids' shape reminded them of a myth describing the creation of the world. According to the myth, the first dry land rose out of the sea, shaped like a mighty pyramid mountain.

The Egyptian sun-god Ra was often shown wearing a crown shaped like the sun.

Try This! Pyramid Poems

In pyramid-shaped poetry, the words are not arranged in lines. They do not rhyme, and they do not usually have a rhythm. Instead, they are written down to make a picture of a pyramid.

Can you write a poem about pyramids, shaped like a pyramid? Here is an example, to start you thinking. See if you can do better!

**A
peak
pointing up.
Sloping sides of
strong stones, standing
balanced on a broad base.
Flat foundations fixed firm for ever.**

Secondly, the sloping sides of the pyramids made the Egyptians think of the sun's slanting rays. Their sun-god, Ra, was mighty creator and protector of their land so the pyramids came to symbolise Ra.

Thirdly, pyramids were like stairways, linking earth to heaven. The Egyptians believed that pyramid-tombs helped a dead pharaoh's spirit climb up into the sky, to join the gods.

The Egyptian sun-god Ra was often shown wearing a crown shaped like the sun.

Pyramid diagrams

Pyramid shapes can also be used by students and scientists to display many different kinds of information. Here is an example:

Pyramid of Life

Here information is represented in a visual pyramid form. The pyramid shape gives an impression of elements stacking up from the smallest element, an atom, which is at the peak of the pyramid through various stages to the largest element, which is shown at the bottom.

atom

molecule

cells

muscle

muscle system

organism

ecosystem

The Great Pyramid

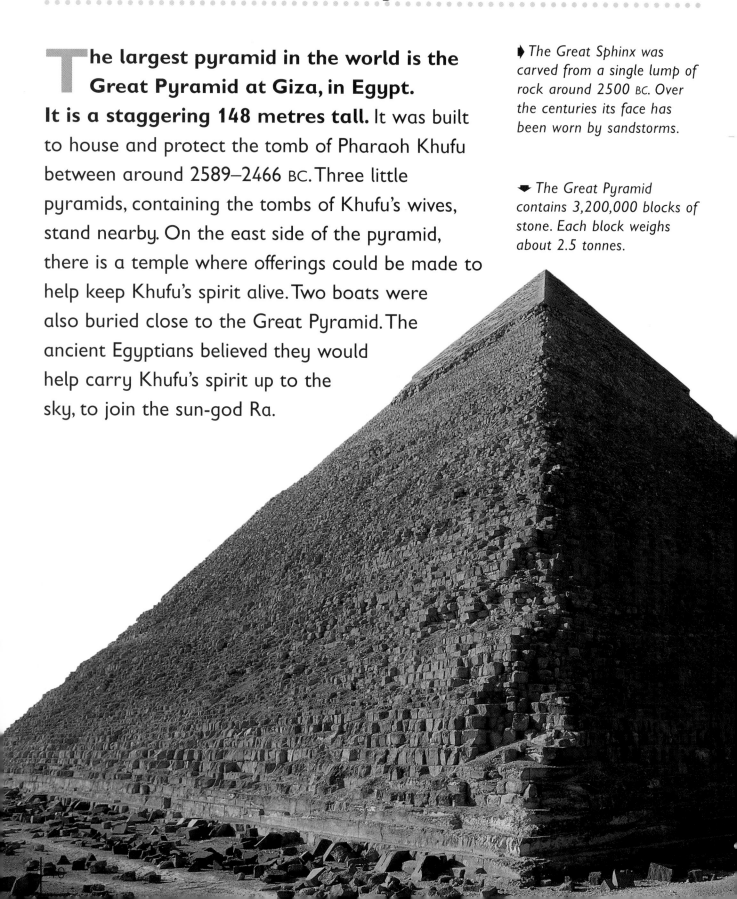

The largest pyramid in the world is the **Great Pyramid at Giza, in Egypt. It is a staggering 148 metres tall.** It was built to house and protect the tomb of Pharaoh Khufu between around 2589–2466 BC. Three little pyramids, containing the tombs of Khufu's wives, stand nearby. On the east side of the pyramid, there is a temple where offerings could be made to help keep Khufu's spirit alive. Two boats were also buried close to the Great Pyramid. The ancient Egyptians believed they would help carry Khufu's spirit up to the sky, to join the sun-god Ra.

▶ *The Great Sphinx was carved from a single lump of rock around 2500 BC. Over the centuries its face has been worn by sandstorms.*

➥ *The Great Pyramid contains 3,200,000 blocks of stone. Each block weighs about 2.5 tonnes.*

The Sphinx

According to ancient mythology, the Sphinx was a monster with the head of a man and the body of a lion. It was a symbol of the pharaoh's royal power. A huge Sphinx statue was built close to the Great Pyramid at Giza, to guard the pharaoh's tomb. It faced East, towards the rising Sun. For the Egyptians, the East where the sun rose was a sign of re-birth and new life.

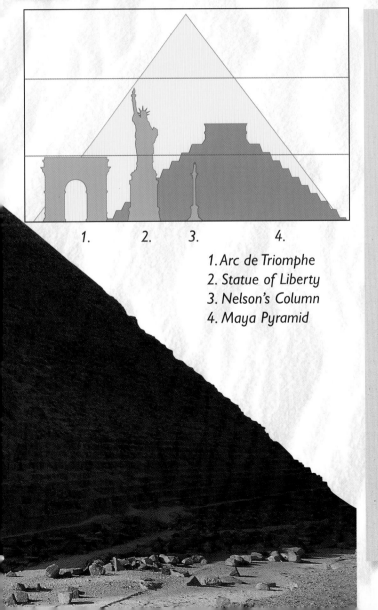

1. Arc de Triomphe
2. Statue of Liberty
3. Nelson's Column
4. Maya Pyramid

Number work

Look at the diagram of the Great Pyramid and other big buildings (left).

Use the information it contains to answer the following questions:

1) The Great Pyramid is 148 m tall. How much taller is it than:
   • The Arc de Triomphe at 49.5 m?
   • The Statue of Liberty at 92 m?
   • Nelson's Column at 44 m?
   • The Maya pyramid at El Mirador at 70 m?

2) What is the volume of the Great Pyramid? You can work it out this way.

   To find the volume of a pyramid multiply:

   its height x area of its base x 0.333

   • The height of the Great Pyramid is 148 m
   • The area of the Great Pyramid's base is 230 x 230 metres (52900 square metres).

Check your answers on page 30.

Pyramids round the world

Most people have heard about the pyramids in **Egypt.** But did you know that there are pyramids in many other parts of the world? There are pyramids in Africa, Asia and Central America, for instance. They were also built for religious purposes, mostly to act as tombs. Some had temples nearby, or even on top. A few were made of stone, but most were made of hardened earth.

▲ *This pyramid-shaped tomb in China is sometimes called the Hill of 10,000 Stones.*

➡ *The kings of Kush (in present-day Sudan) were buried under these pyramids of sun-dried mud bricks from around 650–200 BC.*

⬆ *This pyramid-shaped Buddhist temple was built around* AD *1000 at Pagan, a holy city in Burma, Southeast Asia.*

New pyramids

Today, architects all over the world design many different buildings in pyramid shapes. Like pyramid-builders long ago, they want their designs to look grand and impressive. At a practical level, pyramid-shaped buildings are strong, and can let in a lot of light.

▶ *Rare tropical plants grow inside this twentieth-century pyramid glasshouse in Sydney, Australia.*

Stairways to heaven

The world's earliest cities were built around 5000 years ago, in the Middle East. They were situated on fertile ground between two great rivers, in the land that is now Iraq. The biggest buildings in all these early cities were ziggurats – tall pyramid-shaped towers.

How ziggurats began

The first ziggurat temples were little house-shaped buildings, made of mud bricks, standing on top of mounds ('ziggurat' meant 'mound'). Over the years, new temples were built on top of earlier mounds, growing taller and taller every time. In this way, ziggurats turned into huge pyramid-shaped towers, with stepped sides and temples on top. Temples shaped like ziggurats can still be found in many parts of the world today, particularly Southeast Asia.

This ziggurat was built around 2500 BC in Ur a rich city in the Middle East.

THE TOWER OF BABEL

Many people have heard the Bible story about Noah and his Ark. But did you know that there was another story about Noah's family and a big building project? Here it is:

Noah's sons planned a huge tower. They hoped it would reach all the way to Heaven. They asked people from the different countries in the world to help them build it. But God did not want the tower built. He thought that Noah's sons were too proud and ambitious. They were trying to equal God. So, whenever gangs of workmen arrived at the tower building site, God turned their speech into silly nonsense sounds. Because no-one could understand each other, they could not work together as a team and the tower was never finished.

Like many other Bible stories, this story was written to give a moral message – don't be too proud and ambitious and don't try to be God. But archaeologists think that it may also contain some hidden history. The Jewish scholars who wrote down the Bible stories knew about ziggurats. They may even have seen one of the greatest, the temple of the god Marduk, in the city of Babylon. It was 90 metres high. They called Noah's sons' tower 'the Tower of Babel', after the biggest building they knew. Today, the word 'babble' is used to mean 'nonsense' or 'words that make no sense'.

Maya monuments

The Maya are a Native American people who live in Central American rainforest lands. From AD 250–900 they ruled a splendid civilisation. At the centre of each city stood huge pyramid-shaped buildings. They were made of pounded earth and rubble covered with carved plaster.

Pleasing the gods

These pyramids were temples where sacrifices were offered to the gods. They were also royal tombs, with burial chambers deep inside. The Maya believed that kings who had died were still able to help the cities they once ruled. So they left offerings at their tombs, hoping to be helped in return.

➡ *More than 1200 years ago when this Maya temple was first built, it would have been painted red to symbolise life and blood.*

King Pacal

Pacal was a Maya king from AD 615–683. When he died, his body was dressed in a jade mask because Maya people believed jade stopped dead bodies from rotting. He was buried in a splendid pyramid-shaped tomb. When Maya power collapsed, around AD 900, it became overgrown by plants and lay hidden until it was rediscovered in the 1950s. Today, it is known as the 'Temple of the Inscriptions', because it is decorated with carvings and picture-writing, showing scenes from Pacal's life.

▶ *King Pacal's jade burial mask.*

Try This! Make a Maya mosaic mask

YOU WILL NEED:

- **piece of thin card about 20 cm x 20 cm**
- **about 50 cm elastic**
- **hole punch**
- **scissors**
- **pen or pencil**
- **scraps of green, white and black paper**
- **glue and brush**
- **varnish and brush**

1 *Draw a face shape on the card. Add eyes, nose and mouth.*

2 *Cut out the face shape. Make little holes for seeing at the eyes, and for breathing at the nose and mouth. Punch two holes on each side of the face shape, about level with the eyes.*

3 *Stick scraps of green paper all over the face shape, to look like a mosaic. (You can cut these scraps, or tear them.) Use scraps of black and white paper to show the eyes and the teeth.*

4 *When the face-shape is completely covered with paper mosaic, paint it all over with varnish. Leave it to dry completely.*

5 *Fasten the elastic through the holes in the face shape. Ask a friend to help you make it tighter or looser, until it is comfortable to wear.*

YOU CAN TRY THIS!

The Aztecs

The Aztec people lived in Mexico. From around AD 1345 to 1521 they ruled a great empire. Their capital city, Tenochtitlan, was one of the largest and most powerful anywhere in the world.

Places of worship

The Aztecs believed that Tenochtitlan stood on a holy site in the middle of the world. So they built massive pyramid-temples at its centre, to worship their gods. Each temple was topped with a shrine (holy room) containing a giant statue of a god. The walls inside were decorated with painting and carvings. A stone altar, for human sacrifices, stood outside.

▶ A picture from an Aztec book, or codex, showing a scene of human sacrifice on the steps of a temple.

Treasure troves

The biggest pyramid-temple in Tenochtitlan was dedicated to the Aztecs' two most important gods, Tlaloc (god of life-giving rain) and Huitzilopochtli (god of war). Unlike many other pyramids, Aztec temples were not tombs. But thousands of valuable objects were buried there, as offerings to the gods.

↑ This ornate mosaic carving of a god once formed the handle of an Aztec knife. It would have been a precious possession, used for making human sacrifices to the gods.

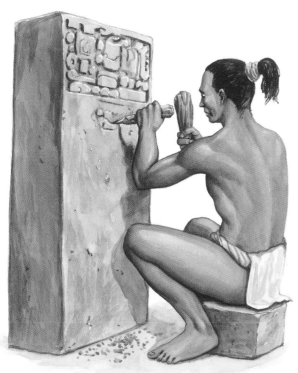

◀ An Aztec scribe carves pictograms in stone.

Writing in pictures

Aztec scribes made a type of folding book called a codex (plural codices), to record events, the names of kings, and observations of the planets and stars. Codices were written in pictograms (picture-script). The Aztecs did not use letters, and had a system of dots to represent numbers. Some Aztec pictograms were little pictures of things. Some stood for ideas. Some were pictures of things that sounded like words it was difficult to draw.

Try This!

Try to invent some pictograms for things we have today that the Aztecs would not have known, for example, planes, telephones, television, the Internet.

YOU CAN TRY THIS!

Try This! Make an Aztec drink

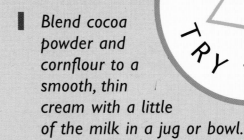

YOU CAN TRY THIS!

Central American people, like the **Maya and the Aztecs, were the first to discover cocoa pods, the raw materials for chocolate.** But they did not make them into chocolate bars. Instead, they enjoyed thick, frothy chocolate drinks flavoured with vanilla, honey and cinnamon. This recipe makes four servings. The Aztecs would not have used milk. They would have crushed cocoa beans to produce a dark milky liquid.

YOU WILL NEED:

- **500 ml milk**
- **2 teaspoons cocoa powder**
- **2 level teaspoons cornflour**
- **1 level tablespoon runny honey**
- **2 level tablespoons grated chocolate (or crushed chocolate flake bar)**
- **Saucepan (NOT non-stick), whisk, heatproof one-litre jug or bowl, grater, heatproof stand.**

plus, if liked:
- **2 drops vanilla essence or**
- **half a level teaspoon powdered cinnamon or more runny honey, to taste**

1 *Blend cocoa powder and cornflour to a smooth, thin cream with a little of the milk in a jug or bowl.*

2 *Grate the chocolate, or crush the chocolate flake bar and put this to one side to use later.*

ASK AN ADULT TO HELP YOU WITH STEPS 3 – 6

3 *Gently heat the rest of the milk to boiling point in a saucepan. Pour about one-third of it into the cocoa and cornflour mixture in a jug or bowl. Whisk very well.*

4 *Pour cocoa, cornflour and milk mixture into the hot milk in the saucepan. Bring back to boiling point, stirring all the time.*

5 *Take saucepan off the heat and place it on heatproof stand. Add honey (plus cinnamon, vanilla essence or extra honey, if using) and whisk mixture very well until frothy.*

6 *Pour at once into mugs, and sprinkle with grated chocolate.*

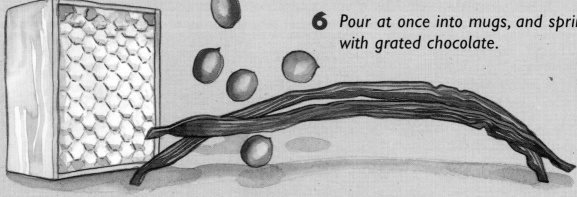

Pyramids today

Modern pyramid buildings are not temples nor tombs. They can be hotels or apartment blocks and, unlike ancient pyramids, they are built to impress anyone who sees them.

▶ A modern pyramid-shaped church in Norway. Its structure combines the standard pyramid shape with the Christian cross.

▲ The sturdy pyramid shape of this skyscraper in San Francisco helps it to withstand earthquakes.

A popular shape

People often find pyramid shapes beautiful and satisfying to look at – even though they can't always explain the attraction. There are pyramid shapes all around us, sometimes in unexpected places. Pyramid-shapes are used for packaging and as decoration. Sometimes, furniture and useful scientific instruments are also pyramid-shaped, for example metronomes used for counting musical beats. Pyramid shapes are stable, as well as strong, so they appeal to manufacturers for a variety of uses.

⬆ Light and elegant, this glass pyramid provides extra space for exhibitions at the famous Louvre museum in Paris, France.

⬆ The fun design of this pyramid and sphinx was chosen for an amusement centre in Las Vegas, USA.

Try This!

Spot the pyramid!

How many pyramid shapes can you find in your home, school, or local shopping centre? Why do you think the people who made them chose pyramid shapes for their designs? Make a list of as many reasons as you can think of.

Try This! Pyramid structures

YOU WILL NEED:

- **9 strips of thin card, about 2 cm x 10 cm, and two strips of card about 2 cm x 5 cm**
- **paper clips**
- **hole punch**
- **scissors**

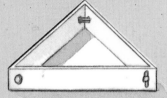

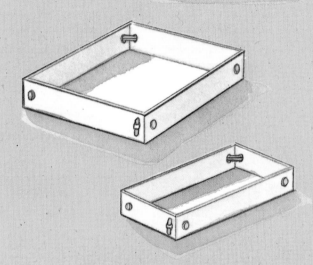

Investigate pyramid structures. They are very strong. This is because their sides are triangle-shaped. Try this experiment to prove the point.

1 *Punch a hole in each end of each card strip.*

2 *Join them together with paper fasteners to make a square, a rectangle and a triangle, as shown.*

3 *Test their strength by gently pulling their sides.*

4 *Which keeps its shape, and which goes out of shape, when you pull?*

Your experiment has shown that the triangle is the most difficult to pull out of shape. It is stronger than the rectangle or the square. Pyramids are also very stable. They are well-balanced and unlikely to tip over. This is because most of their weight is at the base.

YOU CAN TRY THIS!

Inspired by ancient pyramids, this monument in Cairo, Egypt, was built to honour the country's President Sadat who died in 1981.

Magic and mystery

For the past 200 years, people have claimed that pyramids contain hidden, mysterious knowledge, or that they hold the key to understanding how the whole universe works. They have also claimed that sitting inside pyramids, or holding pyramid-shaped crystals, can bring healing. These claims have never been proved true.

A detail of the fascinating writing inside the Pyramid of Saqqarah, Egypt.

An ancient tradition

This tradition of myth and mystery surrounding pyramids is not new. In ancient Egypt, the walls inside pyramids were decorated with the words of magic spells and with pictures of dead people's spirits travelling through the underworld.

Pyramids and the planets

In Central America, kings and queens climbed to the top of pyramids to meet the spirits of their dead ancestors. Pyramids have also been linked in mysterious ways to astronomy (the study of the sun, moon and stars) and with measuring time.

At Chichen Itza, in Mexico, a huge pyramid-temple built by the Toltec people was very cleverly planned and designed, to make use of the Sun's rays. Twice a year the sunlight strikes the pyramid steps at a special angle, revealing a magic snake pattern carved into the stone.

▲ The pyramid temple at Chichen Itza, Mexico, was built around AD 950. The statue at the front of the temple was built to contain offerings to the gods.

Pyramid patterns

Pyramid patterns can be made by artists. They are exciting, dramatic, and sometimes fun. But many pyramid patterns are made by nature. We can see them in big landscape features, such as mountains and lakes, and in small natural things, like crystals and flowers.

◀ Beautiful Mount Pyramid reflected in the still waters of Lake Patricia, Canada.

Pyramids in danger

Today, many ancient Egyptian pyramids are in danger. Big cities and busy roads have been built nearby. Pollution from fires, factories and the motor engines of passing traffic is seriously damaging their stonework.

▲ A dark cloud of polluted air hangs over the city of Cairo close to some of Egypt's ancient pyramids.

▶ Egyptian craftsmen make copies of fragile paintings from Egyptian tombs. They will be displayed in museums so that visitors can see them without harming the originals.

Pyramid protection

Too many tourists are also putting the pyramids in danger. Over time, their feet are wearing away the ground around the pyramids and other nearby monuments. Perspiration from their bodies and the moisture they breathe out are also damaging the delicate wall paintings inside many pyramid tombs.

International organisations are working together with Egyptian experts to try to preserve the pyramids for future generations to enjoy. If something is not done soon, there is a serious risk that these ancient monuments will crumble to dust and disappear for ever.

▲ *These magic spells written inside an Egyptian pyramid might be worn away and lost for ever unless visitors are kept out.*

What's more...

A pyramid of people

Have you ever seen a team of acrobats making a 'human pyramid'? They balance on each other's shoulders to make a pyramid shape. The heaviest and strongest stand at the bottom of the pyramid, while the lightest and most agile somersaults to the top. Sometimes, the acrobats make their pyramid while balancing on horses galloping round and round a circus ring.

◀ Acrobats in India form a human pyramid at a religious festival honouring the Hindu god Krishna.

YOU WILL NEED:

For the electrical element:
- **1 x empty cereal packet**
- **Paper fasteners**
- **Paper clips**
- **1 x battery – type 1203**
- **1 x screw in torch bulb – 4-5 volt**
- **Sticky tape**
- **Thin insulated wire**

For the pyramid:
- **Non-inflammable glue**
- **A square of card, about 50 cm x 50 cm**
- **Scissors**

Try this! Make a pyramid light

To make the pyramid:

1 *Fold the square of card diagonally twice, from corner to corner to make 4 triangle shapes.*

2 *Cut to the middle of the square along one fold.*

3 *Fold the triangle next to the cut inside the one beside it. Glue the two together and leave to dry.*

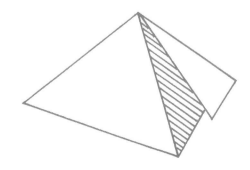

To make the electrical element:

1 Measure and mark this shape on the flattened cereal packet, then cut it out.

2 Carefully score the lines (ask an adult to help you do this). Bend the edges over to form a box shape. Tape the edges together to keep it in shape.

3 Press three paper fasteners through the top of the box – one in the middle and two to one side as shown. Pass one fastener through the thin end of a paperclip. Do not bend the ends over yet. Cut two slits right through the card at either side of the central fastener.

4 Cut out the shape shown from the remaining cardboard and score along the lines (ask an adult to help you). Make a hole in the centre. Bend a paper clip and place it over the hole.

5 Push the end of the bulb through the paper clip and the hole. Bend the card along the scored lines. Push the tabs on the bulb holder

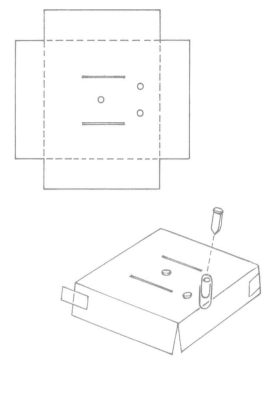

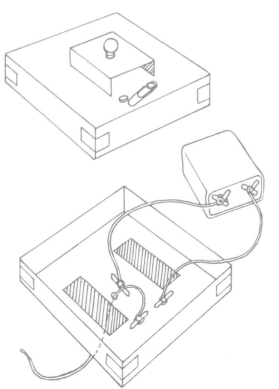

into the slits on the cardboard base until the grey tip of the bulb touches the central paper fastener, otherwise the lamp will not work. Bend over the backs and tape into position.

[Attach this wire to the paper clip on the bulb by removing the insulation and wrapping it round the clip after passing through the top].

6 Attach the wires to the back of the fasteners by removing 15mm of insulation and wrapping round tabs of paper fasteners and then bending the tabs flat. Attach the wires to the battery by the same method as for the bulb using paperclips and then tape the battery into the bottom of the box.

Finally, switch the circuit on. Carefully put your paper pyramid over the lighted circuit. You have a pyramid light.

Glossary

agile: Lively and quick-moving.

ancestors: Parents, grandparents and other close family members who lived long ago.

apex: The highest point of a pyramid.

astronomy: The scientific study of the sun, moon, planets and stars.

base: The lowest part of a pyramid; the part that touches the ground.

burial chamber: A room where a dead body is buried.

cacao: A tropical tree. Its seed pods are used to make chocolate and cocoa.

capstone: The stone right at the very top of a pyramid.

casing: Slabs of stone used as the outer covering of a pyramid.

codex: (plural: codices) Aztec folding books, written in picture-writing.

core: The inner part of a pyramid. face; one of the sloping sides of a pyramid.

foundation: The strong base on which a pyramid (or other building) is constructed.

funeral temples: Buildings close to tombs where prayers were said and offerings were made to the gods and to the spirit of the dead person buried nearby.

Answers

p. 11 The Great Pyramid is:
98.5 m taller than the Arc de Triomphe; 56 m taller than the Statue of Liberty; 104 m taller than Nelson's Column; 78 m taller than the Maya pyramid. Its volume is 2,6071,236.6 cubic metres.

Glossary

intrigued: Made very interested.

mastabas: Tombs built in Egypt about 5000 years ago. They look like low, flat boxes or benches made from bricks.

metronome: An instrument used to beat time in music. It makes a tick-tock sound, like a clock.

pharaohs: The kings who ruled ancient Egypt, from around 3000 BC to 30 BC. The Egyptians believed that their pharaohs had god-like powers.

pictograms: Little pictures of people, places, things and ideas used by some ancient civilisations, including the Aztecs, as a way of writing.

rubble: Rough lumps of brick and stone.

sacrifices: Animals or people killed as offerings to the gods.

shrine: A holy place or a holy room, a tomb or the place where someone is buried.

triangles: Three-sided shapes.

tripods: Three-legged stands.

ziggurat: Tall building in Mesopotamia (present-day Iraq). A ziggurat is made of a number of square platforms, one on top of the other like steps.

Index